EARTH

BY JEFFREY ZUEHLKE

LERNER PUBLICATIONS COMPANY · MINNEAPOLIS

Lerner Publications Company
A division of Lerner Publishing Group, Inc.
241 First Avenue North
Minneapolis, MN 55401 U.S.A.

Website address: www.lernerbooks.com

Library of Congress Cataloging-in-Publication Data

Zuehlke, Jeffrey, 1968–
  Earth / by Jeffrey Zuehlke.
    p.   cm. — (Early bird astronomy)
  Includes index.
  ISBN 978-0-7613-4149-9 (lib. bdg. : alk. paper)
  1. Earth—Juvenile literature. I. Title.
QB631.4.Z84 2010
525—dc22   2008048911

Manufactured in the United States of America
1 2 3 4 5 6 – BP – 15 14 13 12 11 10

CONTENTS

BE A WORD DETECTIVE

Can you find these words as you read about Earth? Be a detective and try to figure out what they mean. You can turn to the glossary on page 46 for help.

astronauts	mantle	solar system
atmosphere	meteorites	spacecraft
axis	molten	temperature
core	orbit	volcanoes
crater	rotate	
elliptical	satellites	

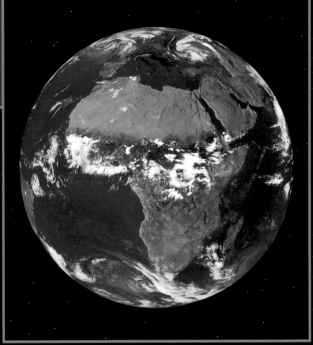

CHAPTER 1
OUR HOME PLANET

Have you seen this planet before? This is Earth. It is home to you and everyone you know. Billions of people live on this planet. Billions more plants and animals live here too. That makes Earth a special planet. As far as we know, no other planet has living beings on it.

planets do not? Our planet has everything creatures need to live. It has water. It has air we can breathe.

People enjoy the bright sunshine and warm temperatures on a beach. Earth's water and air make it an ideal place for living things.

The Sun shines down on a lake in Oregon. We need the Sun's light and warmth.

Earth has warmth too. Gases covering the planet hold in heat from the Sun. That keeps our planet warm. But not too warm. Some planets are much too cold to support life. Others are much too hot. Earth is just the right temperature to support life.

We can study Earth in our own backyard. But scientists have also learned about Earth by studying space. They have learned how other planets are different from ours. Learning more about space helps us understand why our planet is one of a kind.

Studying space has allowed us to learn a lot about Earth.

Kuiper belt

Neptune

Pluto

Uranus

Saturn

Jupiter

CHAPTER 2
EARTH AND ITS NEIGHBORS

Earth shares its neighborhood in space with
many other planets. Earth is part of the solar
system. The solar system includes the Sun
and eight planets. It also includes rocks called
asteroids. Dwarf planets are part of the solar
system too. Dwarf planets are smaller than the
eight main planets.

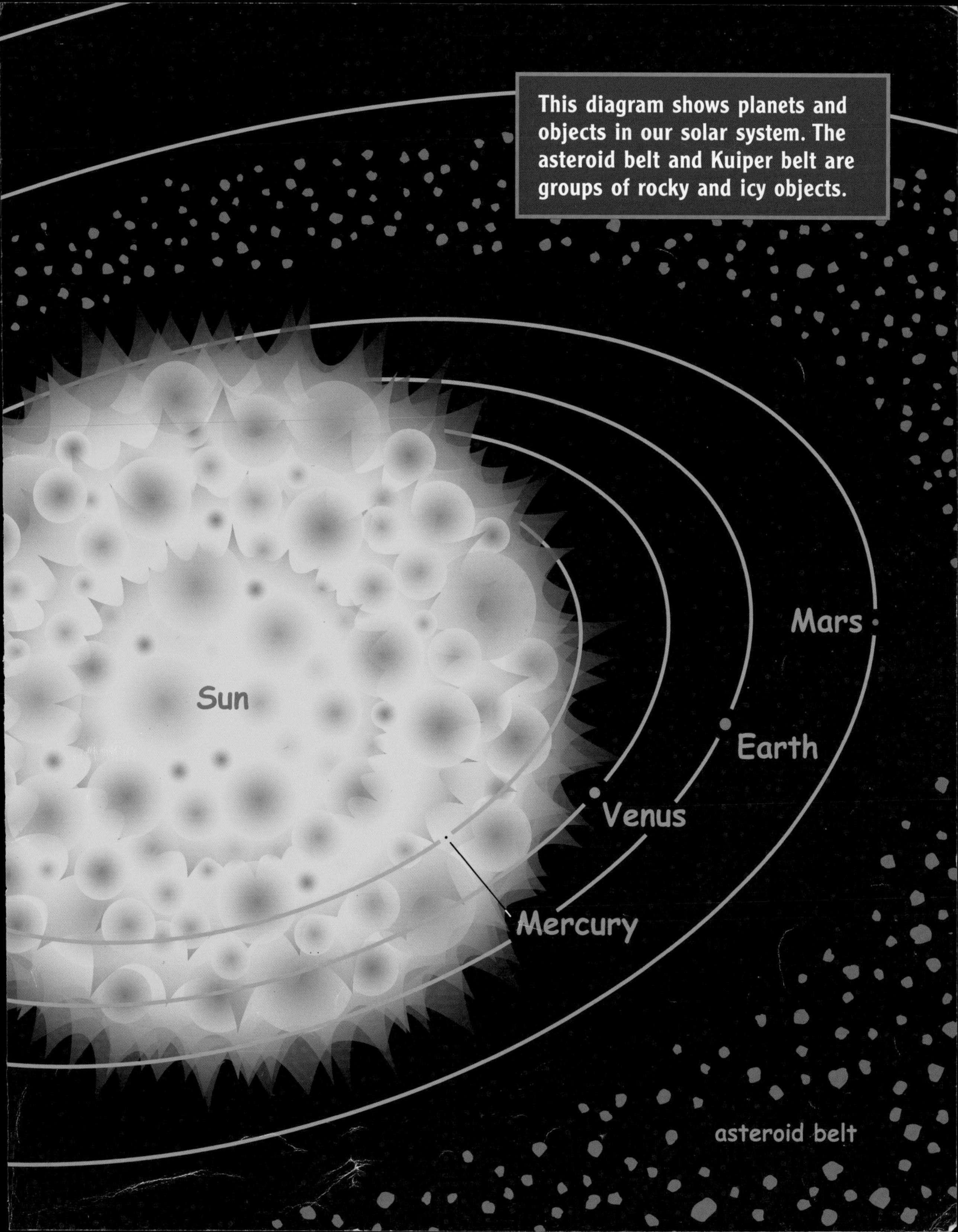

This diagram shows planets and objects in our solar system. The asteroid belt and Kuiper belt are groups of rocky and icy objects.

Mars

Earth

Venus

Sun

Mercury

asteroid belt

The Sun lies at the center of the solar system. The planets closest to the Sun are Mercury, Venus, Earth, and Mars. These planets are made mostly of solid rock. Scientists call them the rocky planets.

Mercury, Venus, Earth, and Mars are made of rock. Some parts of Earth's surface are very rocky, such as this valley in Utah. Other parts are covered by soil.

Neptune, Uranus, Saturn, and Jupiter (LEFT TO RIGHT) are gas planets. They are much larger than the rocky planets.

Jupiter, Saturn, Uranus, and Neptune are called gas giants. They are mostly made of gas. They are the largest planets in the solar system. They are also farthest from the Sun.

This picture shows the eight planets in our solar system. The Sun appears on the left, and the dwarf planet Pluto is on the right. This picture shows the size of each planet compared to others.

Earth is the largest of the rocky planets. It is the fifth-largest planet in the solar system. Earth is nearly 8,000 miles (12,800 kilometers) wide. But our planet is much smaller than the gas giants. More than 1,000 Earths could fit inside Jupiter, the biggest planet.

Earth is the third planet from the Sun. The Sun is about 93 million miles (150 million km) away from Earth. To travel that far on Earth, you would have to circle the globe 3,733 times!

The Sun may be very far from Earth, but its rays warm the planet. Deserts like the Sahara get very hot.

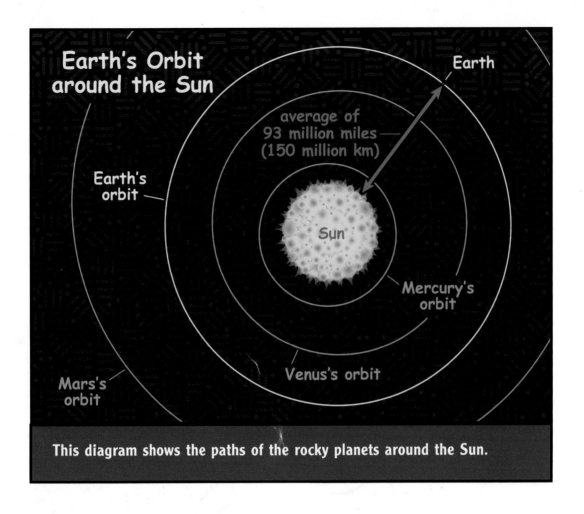

Earth's Orbit around the Sun

Earth

average of 93 million miles (150 million km)

Earth's orbit

Sun

Mercury's orbit

Venus's orbit

Mars's orbit

This diagram shows the paths of the rocky planets around the Sun.

Each planet follows its own path around the Sun. The path is called an orbit. The orbits are a little bit elliptical (ee-LIHP-tih-kuhl). That means they are oval-shaped paths. Earth takes a little more than 365 days to orbit the Sun. One trip around the Sun equals one year.

Planets also rotate (ROH-tayt) as they travel. They spin around like a top. Each planet rotates around its axis (AK-sihs). An axis is an imaginary line that runs through the center of the planet from top to bottom. Earth's axis is tilted. So Earth leans to one side as it spins. It rotates all the way around in 24 hours. That's exactly one day.

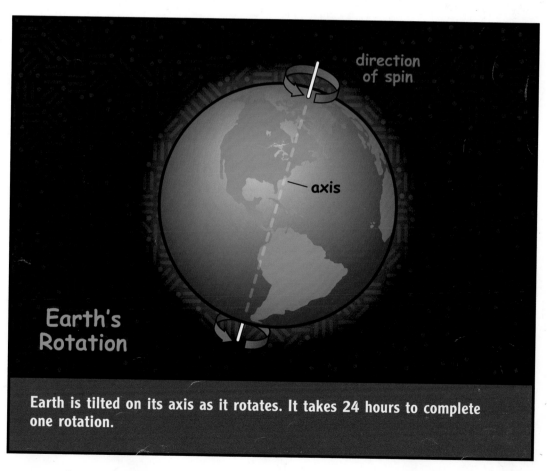

direction of spin

axis

Earth's Rotation

Earth is tilted on its axis as it rotates. It takes 24 hours to complete one rotation.

The blue sky you see is made up of gases. What gases are in Earth's air?

CHAPTER 3
EARTH UP CLOSE

Look up at the blue sky. You are looking at Earth's atmosphere (AT-muhs-feer). The atmosphere is a blanket of gases that surrounds the planet. These gases are mostly nitrogen and oxygen. People and animals breathe oxygen. Plants use oxygen to grow. Water droplets, dust, and carbon dioxide and other gases also make up a tiny part of the atmosphere.

The Sun's heat keeps the atmosphere moving. The Sun warms Earth's surface. The surface warms the air above it. This warm air rises. It cools as it moves upward. Colder air sinks to replace the warm air. The gases in the atmosphere are always rising and falling in this way. This is how weather is created.

Cold air meeting rising warm air can cause storms and strong winds.

Earth's weather includes wind, clouds, rain, snow, and storms. The movement of gases creates wind. Groups of tiny water droplets in the air form clouds. When the droplets join together, they get too heavy to stay in the air. Then clouds release the water as rain or snow. Wind and moisture together can create storms.

This photo of Earth shows storms around the planet. You can see a swirling hurricane on the southern coast of the United States (UPPER RIGHT).

Antarctica, which covers the South Pole, is one of the coldest places on Earth. The poles get less of the Sun's heat than anywhere else.

The gases in the atmosphere hold in the Sun's heat. They protect the planet from the cold of space. Our atmosphere also keeps Earth from getting too hot. It blocks the Sun's hottest rays. The hottest deserts on Earth can reach 136°F (58°C). The coldest parts of Earth can reach a bone-chilling –126°F (–88°C). Most of Earth is somewhere in between.

Oceans cover much of Earth's surface. This photo of the planet shows North America and South America, as well as the Pacific and Atlantic oceans.

Below the atmosphere is Earth's surface. Oceans of salt water cover about 70 percent of Earth. Seven continents and many smaller islands take up the rest of the surface. Mountains, plains, and rolling hills stretch across the land. Rivers and lakes on the continents hold freshwater for drinking. Mountains of ice called glaciers cover some of Earth's coldest land areas.

Under the surface, most of Earth is rock and metal. Several layers make up our planet. The outside layer is called the crust. Earth's crust is thicker in some places and thinner in others. The crust under the oceans is only about 5 miles (8 km) thick. Under continents, it can be up to 25 miles (40 km) thick.

The ground in this part of California split along a crack in Earth's crust.

Earth's crust is made up of about a dozen pieces called plates. These pieces move little by little. When plate edges rub together, they cause earthquakes and volcanoes. Over millions of years, plates pushing against one another can create mountains. Earth's surface is always changing because of its moving plates.

Plate edges rubbing against one another can cause volcanoes to erupt.

The green line running down the middle of the Atlantic Ocean shows the Mid-Atlantic Ridge. It is a ridge of new crust under the ocean. It formed as two plates moved apart.

Earth's plates move by floating on a thick layer below the crust. This layer is the mantle. Earth's mantle is made of hot, puttylike molten rock. This melted rock flows very slowly. It causes the plates to shift. If two plates move apart, it flows into gaps and forms new crust. The mantle is about 1,800 miles (2,880 km) deep.

Beneath the mantle is the center of Earth, called the core. The core is about 2,200 miles (3,520 km) wide. It is made up of metal that is very hot. The outer part of the core is liquid. But the inner part is solid. The hottest part of the core may be about 12,600°F (7,000°C).

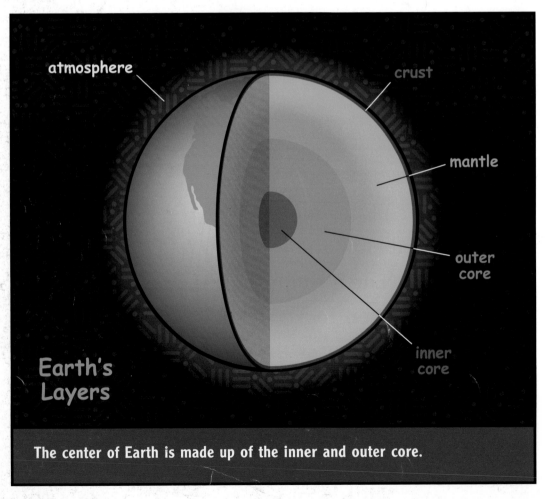

Earth's Layers

atmosphere

crust

mantle

outer core

inner core

The center of Earth is made up of the inner and outer core.

A full moon hangs in the night sky. Which is bigger, the Moon or Earth?

CHAPTER 4

EARTH'S CLOSEST NEIGHBOR

Everyone knows about Earth's closest neighbor. We see it in the sky almost every night. It is the Moon.

The Moon is much smaller than Earth. It is about 2,160 miles (3,475 km) wide. About 50 moons would fit inside Earth.

The Moon looks small when shown side by side with Earth. (It is actually much farther from Earth than shown here.)

Our Moon orbits Earth, just as Earth orbits the Sun. The Moon takes about 27 days to travel around Earth.

Like our planet, the Moon also rotates. But it rotates much more slowly than Earth. The Moon takes a little more than 27 days to turn all the way around. Since it travels around Earth in the same amount of time, the same side of the Moon always faces us.

From night to night, the Moon seems to change shape. Sometimes we can see the full moon. Other times, it looks as if it has been cut in half. The Moon's shape seems to change just a little each night. Over about one month, it grows into a full moon and then gets smaller and disappears again.

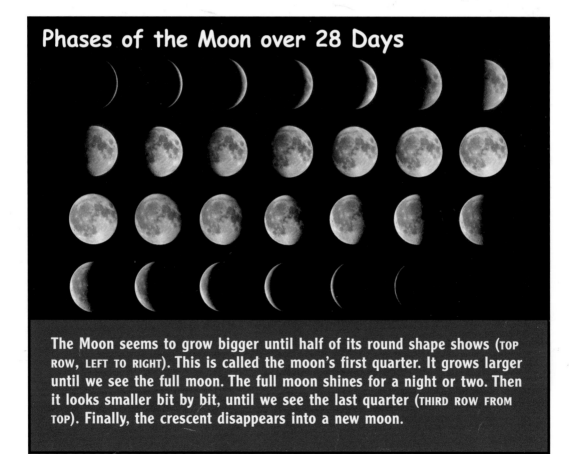

Phases of the Moon over 28 Days

The Moon seems to grow bigger until half of its round shape shows (TOP ROW, LEFT TO RIGHT). This is called the moon's first quarter. It grows larger until we see the full moon. The full moon shines for a night or two. Then it looks smaller bit by bit, until we see the last quarter (THIRD ROW FROM TOP). Finally, the crescent disappears into a new moon.

We see only the parts of the Moon that are lit by the Sun. As the Moon travels around Earth, sunlight hits the Moon from different directions. When it hits the side of the Moon facing Earth, we see a full moon. If it mostly lights the side facing away from Earth, we see only a sliver.

On one night in February 2008, the Moon looked red. That's because the Sun, Earth, and the Moon were all lined up. Earth blocked direct sunlight from reaching the Moon. (This is called a lunar eclipse.) Some light passed through Earth's atmosphere and lit the Moon red.

The Moon is closer to Earth than any planets are. But it is still very far away.

The Moon may not seem far away. But it is very far. Our Moon is 238,855 miles (384,400 km) from Earth. Imagine you could drive from Earth to the Moon in a car going 50 miles (80 km) per hour. It would take nearly 200 days of nonstop driving to get there.

This image shows the gray surface of the Moon. The dark patches are areas filled with lava rock. This is the side of the Moon we see from Earth.

Once you reached the Moon, what would you see? The Moon's surface is mostly gray rocks and dirt. You would see some mountains and many deep valleys. You would also see many craters (KRAY-turs). Craters are bowl-shaped pits in the surface. Some craters are just a few miles wide. The largest ones are more than 1,000 miles wide (1,610 km).

Craters are formed when rocks or ice from space slam into the Moon's surface. These objects are called meteorites (MEE-tee-uh-ryets) and comets (KAH-mehts).

The Moon's surface has craters of many different sizes. These craters are on the side of the Moon that faces away from Earth.

What else would you notice? There is no life on the Moon. The Moon has almost no atmosphere. So there is no air to breathe.

Without an atmosphere, nothing protects the Moon from the Sun's heat. Nothing holds in any of the Sun's warmth either. So the Moon gets very hot and very cold. Sunny parts of the Moon get as hot as 253°F (123°C). Other places get as cold as –387°F (–233°C).

The Moon is seen through a thin layer of Earth's atmosphere. The Moon has no atmosphere of its own.

This photo of Earth rising over the Moon's surface was taken in 1968. When were the first photos of Earth taken?

CHAPTER 5
SPACE MISSIONS FROM EARTH

For thousands of years, no one knew what Earth looked like from space. No one had ever seen photos of Earth until the 1940s.

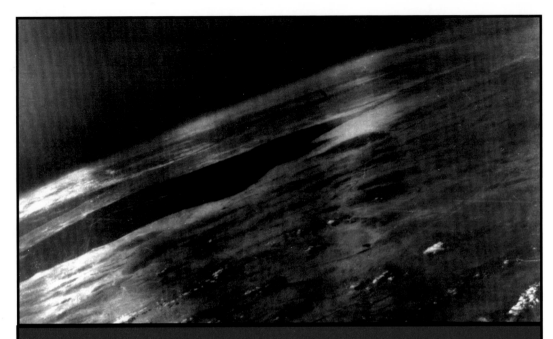

This black-and-white photo was one of the first pictures of Earth as seen from space. It was taken in 1946.

To take pictures of Earth, people had to build machines to fly high above the planet. In 1946, the U.S. Army sent a rocket up into space. The rocket took pictures looking back toward Earth as it shot up and then fell to the ground. These were the first pictures that showed what a part of Earth's surface looks like from space. Over the years, scientists built better spacecraft.

A spacecraft is a vehicle that travels in space. The first spacecraft to orbit Earth was *Sputnik*. It was launched in October 1957. *Sputnik* was a metal ball about the size of a large beach ball. It orbited Earth for 23 days.

In 1961, the first human was sent into space. His name was Yuri Gagarin. Many others have traveled to space since then. People who travel to space are called astronauts (A-struh-nawts).

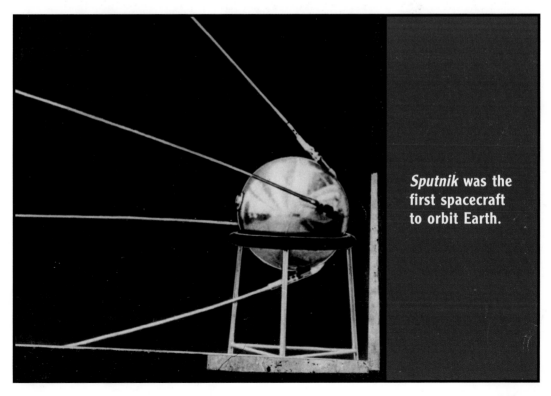

Sputnik was the first spacecraft to orbit Earth.

In 1969, two U.S. astronauts became the first people to walk on the Moon. Their names are Neil Armstrong and Edwin "Buzz" Aldrin. After that, U.S. astronauts made six more trips to walk on the Moon.

Astronaut Buzz Aldrin stands near the U.S. flag that he placed on the Moon in 1969.

Scientists use computers to keep track of spacecraft in orbit.

No one has visited the Moon since 1972. But scientists continue to build spacecraft. Most have no people on board. They are controlled by computers and people on Earth.

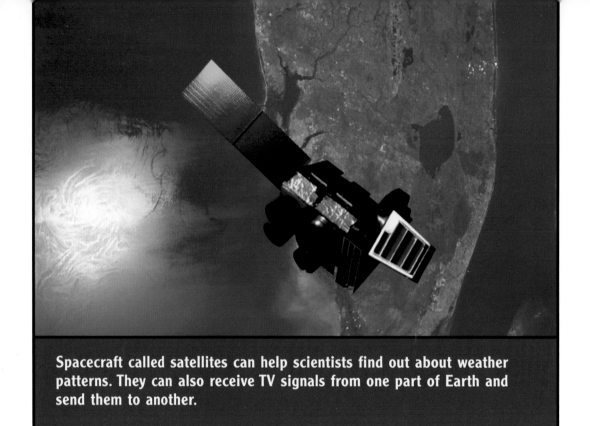

Spacecraft called satellites can help scientists find out about weather patterns. They can also receive TV signals from one part of Earth and send them to another.

Many of these spacecraft are orbiting our planet right now. They are called satellites (SA-tuh-lyets). Satellites do many things. Some take pictures of Earth. Others take pictures of outer space. These satellites tell us many important things about Earth and the solar system. People also use satellites to send information from one part of Earth to another.

Astronauts continue to travel to space. In 1981, two U.S. astronauts flew on the first space shuttle mission. Since then, space shuttles have carried many satellites and other spacecraft into space. Shuttles have even carried supplies to help build space stations.

The space shuttle *Discovery* lifts off in May 2008. The space shuttle is made up of the orbiter, two solid rocket boosters, and the external tank. The orbiter can be used over and over again. It is the part that looks like an airplane.

A space station is a satellite that people live in. It is a place where astronauts can spend days or even months in space.

In 1998, astronauts began building the International Space Station (ISS). Many missions have brought new parts to add to the station. It is the largest space station ever built.

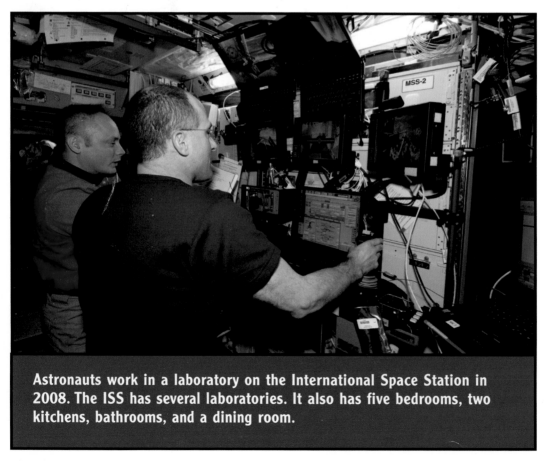

Astronauts work in a laboratory on the International Space Station in 2008. The ISS has several laboratories. It also has five bedrooms, two kitchens, bathrooms, and a dining room.

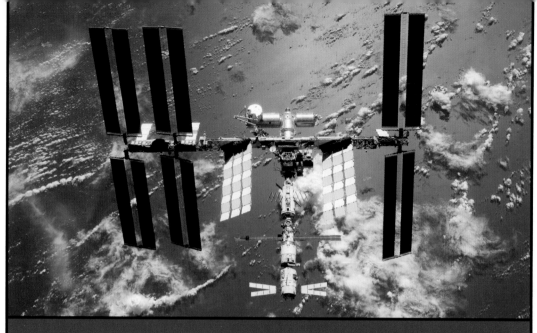

Earth can be seen behind the ISS as the station orbits in space. The ISS orbits 240 miles (386 km) above Earth.

Astronauts are studying many things on the ISS. For example, they use special cameras and sensors to gather new information about Earth's atmosphere.

The ISS is big enough to be seen from Earth. Have you ever spotted the ISS? Keep looking, and you will see it. And maybe someday, you'll have a chance to visit and study our planet from space.

LEARN MORE ABOUT
EARTH

BOOKS

Editors of TIME for Kids and Lisa Jo Rudy. *Planets!* New York: HarperCollins, 2005. Make a visit to each of the planets in our solar system in this book.

Lauw, Darlene. *Earth and the Solar System.* New York: Crabtree Publishing, 2003. Learn more about our home planet and the solar system through activities and experiments.

Storad, Conrad J. *Earth's Crust.* Minneapolis: Lerner Publications Company, 2007. Find out more about Earth's plates and how Earth's crust is always changing.

Zuehlke, Jeffrey. *The Space Shuttle.* Minneapolis: Lerner Publications Company, 2006. Read about the most famous spacecraft ever built.

WEBSITES

The Greenhouse Effect
http://epa.gov/climatechange/kids/greenhouse.html
Find out how Earth's atmosphere keeps our planet the right temperature.

Human Space Flight (HSF)—Realtime Data
http://spaceflight.nasa.gov/realdata/sightings/
Check out the "sighting opportunities" section with an adult to find out when and where to look for the ISS in the sky!

NASA—Students K-4
http://www.nasa.gov/audience/forstudents/k-4/index.html
Click on "Steps to Countdown Storybook" to see how parts of a space shuttle come together before it is launched into orbit.

Solar System Exploration: Planets: Earth: Gallery
http://solarsystem.nasa.gov/planets/profile.cfm?Object=Earth&
Display=Gallery
See what Earth looks like from other planets! You can also view satellite photos and diagrams of Earth and the Moon in space.

GLOSSARY

astronauts (A-struh-nawts): people who travel to outer space

atmosphere (AT-muhs-feer): the layer of gases that surrounds a planet

axis (AK-sihs): an imaginary line that goes through a planet from top to bottom. A planet spins on its axis.

core: the ball-shaped innermost layer of Earth

crater (KRAY-tur): a bowl-shaped pit

elliptical (ee-LIHP-tih-kuhl): oval-shaped

mantle: the thick layer of melted rock that lies beneath Earth's crust

meteorites (MEE-tee-uh-ryets): rocks from outer space that have landed on a planet's surface

molten: melted

orbit: the curved path a planet, moon, or other space object travels in space. To orbit can also mean to travel along this path.

rotate (ROH-tayt): to spin around like a top

satellites: spacecraft that travel around Earth. Moons and other objects that circle larger objects are also called satellites.

solar system: a group of planets and other objects that travel around the Sun

spacecraft: a machine that travels from Earth to outer space

temperature: a measure of hotness or coldness. Temperature is measured in degrees (°) Fahrenheit or Celcius.

volcanoes: places where hot, melted rock flows out of the ground

INDEX

Pages listed in **bold** type refer to photographs.